CONTENTS

Introduction
The Arduous Process of Tax Filing   1
IRS Can't Go Toe to Toe with the Tax Prep Industry   10
The Tax Prep Industry Wants to Make Money Off Americans   20
Disproportionately Audits Poorer Citizens   23
What Could Make It Better?   32

INTRODUCTION

Americans only have to file taxes once a year. For something that only happens once a year it shouldn't take so long, right? Well, wrong. While we only do this once a year it apparently takes Americans approximately 2 billion hours to file taxes each year according to the Federal Register (information provided by Patriot Act with Hasan Minhaj). That's about 12.5 hours per taxpayer. Taxes can take long amounts of time for even the smallest refund. It can take even more time if an individual is audited too. Doesn't sound so easy, does it? It's not, and that's why so many people dread tax season each year.

It also bears the question, why is it so hard to do taxes? To answer that question, you would have to consider the form in which most Americans do their taxes. We should also consider how often Americans are audited. They all play a role in answering the question. So, in this article, I will briefly go over both in order for you to have a better understanding.

THE ARDUOUS PROCESS OF TAX FILING

First off, how do you file taxes? They usually don't teach you how to file taxes in school, so why is it important? The first thing to figure out is whether or not you are required to file a tax return. To find out if you need to file your taxes, you'll need to assess your employment situation. It's easiest when you are employed regularly at some sort of job. If this is the case, you'll have to take your filing status, age, and gross income into account before finding out whether or not you have to file taxes. For example, if you are single, under the age of 65, and have a gross income that exceeds $12,200, you are going to be required to file taxes. In the case that your income is below $12,200, you wouldn't be required to file taxes at all. The IRS has a handy Interactive Tax Assistant Tool that tells you whether or not you need to file a tax return after you answer a few uncomplicated questions.

You might be required to file taxes even if you aren't employed by an organization. Let's say, for instance, that you are self-employed. This means that you are going to get a Form 1099 instead of a W-2. You're going to have to file taxes as long as your net earnings exceed $400. In the case that you don't meet the minimum gross income for your job and you aren't self-employed, you still might have to pay taxes. Individuals who owe the government, such as through household employment taxes or homebuyer's tax credit, will be required to file taxes regardless of their employment status.

There are also special cases in which you would have to file a tax return, including in cases of religious wages, medical savings accounts, and retirement programs. There are plenty of resources online that will help you assess whether or not you are required by law to turn in your taxes on Tax Day. The money that you pay via taxes go back to the government, and they use it in ways that are supposed to better our society. For example, your tax dollars might be used for defense and national security costs, health aid, university research, and road construction.

When it comes to filing taxes, there are typically two methods to choose from. You can either file your own taxes by hand and then mail them to the IRS or you can use an independent software package, such as TurboTax or H&R Block. Filing your taxes by hand may seem daunting at first glance, but there are a few benefits to filing your taxes this way. People who have simple tax returns choose to file their taxes by hand in order to save time and money. Whereas tax software would help you through the process, filing by hand means that you're on your own.

However, that isn't always a bad thing. Perhaps you want an inside look at where your taxes are going without the interference of an automated program telling you what to do or you only have a few assets to worry about. If this is the case, then filing by hand might be the method for you. Many people choose to file their taxes without the help of a tax software program in order to take a stand against the United States' overly complex tax code. Thanks to tax software programs, filing taxes has evolved into an arduous, complicated process. By foregoing companies like TurboTax or TaxSlayer, you can send a message to government officials that says, "We want a simple tax code!" In addition to all of these benefits, filing taxes by hand means that the tax return process will cost you virtually nothing. All you'll have to pay for is the ink and paper that you're writing on. If this sounds like the right method for you, all you have to do is go to IRS.gov and print out the necessary tax return forms.

Let's say that you just want to get your tax return finished as fast as possible. If this is the case, you might want to consider filing with the help of a tax program. Though we'll later discuss the ways in which sites like TurboTax and TaxAct exploit the American people, using a tax program is, nevertheless, the most common way that Americans file taxes. There are a few benefits to using a tax program instead of filing by hand. You are less likely to make a costly error if you use a tax program. Tax programs are designed to limit silly mistakes, whereas people who file by hand are prone to human error. Mistakes on tax forms can cost you money, so tax programs may be the way to go if you're not confident in your tax filing abilities. Another benefit to filing your taxes with a tax program is the amount of time and mental effort that you'll save. A thorough taxpayer would read and understand the *Standard Federal Tax Reporter*, which consists of 70,000 pages and over 10 million words. Definitely not a light read. Of course, most people don't read the tax code in its entirety, but tax programs make it easier by only providing you with the most essential parts of the tax code, which are the parts that are relevant to your specific situation. A downside to using tax programs is the cost. Though many programs will claim to have free versions, there are actually many hidden costs associated with them that we will discuss later in the guide.

In addition to filing by hand and using a tax software, you can also seek the help of a tax preparer. This is a great option if you'd like one-on-one assistance from someone who lives, eats, and breathes taxes, such as a tax preparation firm member or an accountant. If you choose to go this route, the IRS has resources to help you find a trustworthy representative in your area.

Whether you decide to file your taxes by hand or with the help of a tax software program, it's important to start the process with plenty of time to spare. Filing taxes can be a long, unpleasant process, so it's important to start early so that you don't miss the April deadline.

If you are a beginner, here are some helpful tips to make your first tax filing a stress-free success.

The first tip is to know your filing status. What is a filing status? There are five filing statuses: single, married filing separately, married filing jointly, head of household, and qualifying widow(er) with dependent child. Single means that you aren't married. Married filing separately might be a good option for people in marriages who want to be in charge of their own taxes. It also might be the best option financially. Sometimes you'll end up paying less if you file separately than if you file jointly, so it's important to calculate both scenarios before deciding how you will fill in your filing status. Head of household is a special case where someone isn't married but has paid more than half of the cost of maintaining a house with another person. The last filing option, qualifying widow(er) with dependent child, is self-explanatory. Why is it important to choose the right filing status? Well, according to the official IRS website: "It's important to use the right filing status when you file your tax return. The status you choose can affect the amount of tax you owe for the year. It may even determine if you must file a tax return. Keep in mind that your marital status on Dec. 31 is your status for the whole year. Sometimes more than one filing status may apply to you. If that happens, choose the one that allows you to pay the least amount of tax." Choosing the right filing status may be the difference between paying a lot of money and paying a little.

Our second tip is to stay organized. It's important to keep track of your receipts, medical records, and W-2 forms as they arrive so that you can save the time that you would've spent searching for them in the future. Having all of your tax-related files in one place will make the tax filing process come tax time way more efficient and way less aggravating. One way to stay organized is to purchase an accordion file. Using an accordion file is a great way to store your tax documents, as you can separate the sections by year and keep all of your forms in one place. Need to see a tax return from 2013? Just go to your accordion folder and look inside of the section labeled "2013," where you'll find every form from 2013 nice and organized. Easy peasy. You should also label all of your receipts. Writing down why you purchased something right after you buy it will save you from racking your brain later down the road when you can barely even remember buying the thing in the first place. Investing in a receipt scanner may be a wise decision if you're a person who is known for losing things easily. If you own a receipt scanner, you can scan your receipt as soon as you get it and file it away, lessening the chance that you will lose it before tax season.

Also, spreadsheets are always a good idea. Keeping a spreadsheet, either online using a program like Excel or simply using a pen and paper, will help you to calculate items such as your charitable donations throughout the year, which will make summing up your tax deduction much easier. Just as it is beneficial to keep the documents that you need in a safe place, it is also a good idea to shred the documents that you don't need. You can purchase a paper shredder if you want to shred your documents at home or you can find and travel to a local shredding service. Shredding old documents and forms that are no longer needed will help to limit the clutter in your drawers and cabinets, making it easier to find the items that you actually need.

Our third tip is to take advantage of tax deductions. When filing for tax deductions, you have two options. The first is to choose the standard deduction option. What does this standard deduction method mean? According to the official IRS website: "The standard deduction is a specific dollar amount that reduces the amount of income on which you're taxed. Your standard deduction consists of the sum of the basic standard deduction and any additional standard deduction amounts for age and/or blindness. In general, the standard deduction is adjusted each year for inflation and varies according to your filing status, whether you're 65 or older and/or blind, and whether another taxpayer can claim you as a dependent. The standard deduction isn't available to certain taxpayers. You can't take the standard deduction if you itemize your deductions."

Therefore, taking the standard deduction route means that the IRS chooses a deduction amount for you based on your filing status. This might be the best option for you if you don't want to put in the time it takes to calculate itemized tax deductions. Additionally, anyone can take the standard deduction, even if they don't have the expenses associated with itemized deductions, such as medical expenses and charitable donations. For the year 2020, the standard tax deductions were $12,400.00 for single people, $24,800 for married filing jointly, $18,650 for the head of household, and $12,400 for married filing separately.

If your standard deduction exceeds your itemized deduction, you're going to want to choose to take the standard deduction, as the amount you pay on your income will be less. What about itemized deductions?

You should itemize deductions instead of taking the standard deduction "if your allowable itemized deductions are greater than your standard deduction or if you must itemize deductions because you can't use the standard deduction." While standard deductions will be the same for each filing status, itemized deductions are different for each taxpayer. This is because standard deductions are based on your expenses, and your expenses will most certainly differ from other people's expenses. With itemized deductions, you add up all of your deductions from various expenses and then subtract that total from your taxable income. The higher the number is, the better. Some common itemized deductions are mortgage interest, charitable donations, medical expenses, and even gambling losses.

Donating to a charity is one of the most popular ways that people increase their itemized deduction amount. Even donating to a charity has its limitations, though. According to the IRS website: "In general, contributions to charitable organizations may be deducted up to 50 percent of adjusted gross income computed without regard to net operating loss carrybacks. Contributions to certain private foundations, veterans organizations, fraternal societies, and cemetery organizations are limited to 30 percent adjusted gross income (computed without regard to net operating loss carrybacks), however. Tax Exempt Organization Search uses deductibility status codes to indicate these limitations."

Due to the devastations of Covid-19, however, the limitations on the amount of income that can be deducted as a result of charitable donations were temporarily lifted. "In most cases, the amount of charitable cash contributions taxpayers can deduct on Schedule A as an itemized deduction is limited to a percentage (usually 60 percent) of the taxpayer's adjusted gross income (AGI)," says the government official website. "Qualified contributions are not subject to this limitation. Individuals may deduct qualified contributions of up to 100 percent of their adjusted gross income. A corporation may deduct qualified contributions of up to 25 percent of its taxable income. Contributions that exceed that amount can carry over to the next tax year."

Another common type of itemized deduction is medical and dental expenses. "Medical care expenses include payments for the diagnosis, cure, mitigation, treatment, or prevention of disease, or payments for treatments affecting any structure or function of the body." You can only deduct medical expenses that are greater than 7.5% of your adjusted gross income. Some examples of instances where you would be able to deduct medical expenses are payments for nursing home services, payments for dentures and hearing aids, and payments incurred for drug or alcohol rehabilitation.

Medical expenses and charitable donations are just a few of the many expenditures that are eligible for tax deductions, so be sure to review the exhaustive list of itemized deductions in order to determine whether itemized deductions or the standard deduction is the right choice for you.

Our fourth tip is to explore IRS.gov. The United States Government official website has an abundance of resources that will prove extremely helpful when it's time to file taxes. When you first log on to their homepage, you're greeted with many useful links. There are links to places where you can get your refund status, get answers on the advance child tax credit, and get your tax record, among many others. Though it should be more prominently advertised, there's even a box that you can click on that will take you to IRS Free File. Exploring IRS.gov will be especially helpful for first-time tax filers. There are links to pages that tell you how, when, and where to file, as well as tools that will help guide you as you go through the tax filing process. Need a 1040 form? The IRS website has got you covered. Want to know more about the Coronavirus Tax Relief plan? The IRS has a whole page dedicated to Coronavirus Tax Relief updates and policies. Each page even has a "Page Last Reviewed or Updated" insert at the bottom, so you know just how recent the information on the page really is. There is also a section at the bottom of the website titled "Know Your Rights," which is useful to anyone who has questions regarding taxpayer's rights.

Our final tip is to familiarize yourself with the various forms that you might encounter come tax season. There are a few forms that you should be familiar with when preparing to file taxes. Gaining familiarity with these forms prior to filing taxes will streamline the process, making it easier, faster, and less stressful. The first is the W-2 forms. The W-2 form is given to employees by their employers. The form details the wages that the employee earned over the year, as well as the amount of money withheld from the employee's paycheck for the purpose of federal income taxes. The amount of money withheld is important because it is the amount that you are required to subtract from your tax bill. The second form that you should be familiar with is the 1099 form. This form is essential for anyone who does work outside of their principal employers, such as freelance work or self-employment earnings. The 1099 form has another variation called the 1099-INT form. This form is used to report interest income. Any interest-related investments, savings accounts, or expenses will be included in this form. The last tax form that we're going to mention is the 1098 form. For all the students out there, the 1098 form is the one that you're going to want to pay close attention to, as it has to do with student loans. This form will detail all of the interest you've had to pay on your student loans, as well as how much of your student loans are deductible. In addition to student loans, the 1098 form also involves mortgage payments. Of course, this is only a small fraction of the forms that you may receive in the mail come tax return time. It's important to keep all of these forms together and in one place so that you don't lose track of them.

IRS CAN'T GO TOE TO TOE WITH THE TAX PREP INDUSTRY

A vast number of American taxpayers file their taxes online. To be more accurate, 40% of Americans file their taxes online. That means there are millions of Americans turning to tax prep services like Intuit TurboTax, TaxSlayer, and TaxAct. These tax preparation services are so popular among the American people for their simple layout and use that, if the IRS wanted to introduce their own free individual tax prep service through their website, it would have a lot of competition.
Actually, the IRS tried to start its own tax software at one point. It was going to be free and easy to use. However, Intuit, the same company that owns TurboTax, decided to partner with them and create their IRS Free File Program. This is supposedly the free tax prep service that Intuit TurboTax offers unlike their Intuit TurboTax Free Edition, which ironically isn't "free".

Intuit has a long history of trying to force consumers to pay for services that they could otherwise get for free. Founded in 1983 by Scott Cook and Tom Proulx, Intuit has a somewhat messy history of lawsuits and is even currently under investigation by the Federal Trade Commission. Scott Cook came up with the idea for

Intuit after hearing his wife complain about how difficult it was to pay the bills by hand. At the time, Cook had been working for the management consulting firm Bain & Company, where he had been gaining valuable knowledge related to marketing and product development. He asked the question, "What if there was a way to manage finances via online software?" From there, and along with the help of computer programmer and Stanford graduate Tom Proulx, Cook launched Intuit. Today, Cook has a net worth of a whopping $5.3 billion. Instated in 2019, Sasan Goodarzi currently serves as Intuit's Chief Executive Officer. Intuit currently offers products such as TurboTax, QuickBooks, ProConnect, and Credit Karma, as well as many international services.

Cook and Proulx first operated Intuit out of a small room on University Avenue, doing their best to compete with their much bigger, already established competitors. They began by encoding the first version of Quicken into Microsoft's BASIC programming language. Quicken was doing alright, but it still had trouble competing with the big players in the software world, such as Microsoft. When Microsoft launched Microsoft Money in 1991, Quicken had to find a way to make their services more appealing than their competitors. In an attempt to maintain customer loyalty, Inuit offered a $15 rebate coupon that was redeemable on in-store purchases.

A rebate is different from a discount. Rebates are retrospective payments that decrease the amount you pay at a later date. Intuit was the first software company to offer a rebate for its customers. Intuit continued to make business moves, partnering with venture capital firm Kleiner Perkins, diversifying the products offered to consumers, and increasing output and growth year after year. Intuit went public in 1993, making its shares available to purchase by retailers and investors. Intuit acquired Chipsoft, a tax preparation software company, with the money the company made from selling shares. Chipsoft was founded by Michael A. Chipman, who later went on to develop the Intuit-produced software TurboTax.

This proved to be a vital acquisition for Inuit, as the company's valuation reached $2 billion a year later in 1994. Inuit came across a few roadblocks in the latter half of the 1990s, mainly due to increased competition with Microsoft. Intuit continued to push forward, launching new products, making key investments, and amping up the advertisements for Quickbooks and TurboTax. In March of 1999, Intuit acquired Computing Resources Inc. for $200 million, which allowed for improvements in Intuit's QuickBooks software program. Later that year, Intuit bought Rock Financial for $532 million and renamed it Quicken Loans. Quicken Loans is now the largest online mortgage lending company in the world. The 2000s were filled with new acquisitions and investments, all of which improved Intuit's user interface, increased Intuit's available features, and skyrocketed the company's net worth. In 2020, Intuit announced its plans to acquire Credit Karma for a modest $7.1 billion and TradeGecko for $100 million.

Intuit has also engaged in lobbying over the years. Lobbying is an attempt to influence the decisions of government officials and lawmakers. In 2007, Intuit lobbied against the IRS, ensuring that the IRS couldn't set up its own tax preparation software. This forced consumers to file their taxes through services such as TurboTax or H&R Block. They did this because the IRS would've offered their tax software for free, driving customers to switch from Intuit services to the services of the IRS. Steve Ryan was the lawyer who negotiated the deal that prevented the IRS from creating a website for tax-related e-filing. Ryan defended his case by stating: "When the government becomes my competitor, then I have every right to run an ad that says 'Big Brother is watching your keystrokes.'"

According to a 2009 report by the Los Angeles Times, Intuit lobbied for the elimination of a bill that would equip low-income families in California with the ability to file their tax returns free of charge. "Intuit, which makes TurboTax, has spent $618,000 on lobbying in Sacramento since 2007 and donated to the campaigns of 29 of the 40 state senators since 2005," said the reporters at the Los Angeles Times. All of the money that Intuit spent on lobbying went towards the elimination of free tax return services, and it worked. Thanks to companies like TurboTax, the bill that would've allowed free tax filing for low-income families was eventually scrapped.

ProPublica reported in 2013 that Intuit has been fighting against return-free tax filing, which would be a simple, fast, and free alternative to tax preparers and tax software like TurboTax. Notable figures such as President Ronald Reagan and President Barack Obama have supported the idea of return-free tax filing, but it still has yet to be available. This is mainly due to the fact that Intuit has been lobbying against return-free tax filing, spending nearly $12 million in federal lobbying efforts in order to inhibit the IRS from putting out their own tax software. Intuit spokeswoman Julie Miller defended the company's decision to lobby against return-free filing.

"In countries where income taxation is handled from start to finish as a centralized government function, rather than citizen-centric through Voluntary Compliance, the ability for the government to employ the tax system as a channel for implementing economic policy is sharply limited," said Miller in an emailed statement. "Relying on an actual withholding or government reconciliation tax system, eliminating or curtailing citizen participation in the taxation process, has far-reaching implications for accuracy and public tax expenditures, which are often targeted by policymakers to those lower and middle-income citizens with the simplest returns. This, in turn, has implications for accuracy and fairness in taxation itself."

There have been recent reports, however, that Intuit has admitted to opposing return-free filing because it would be detrimental to Intuit's business. Not very helpful for their case. Many have said that Intuit's fears are exaggerated, as filing with the government wouldn't be forced upon taxpayers. "It's voluntary," said chief economist for the President's Economic Recovery Advisory Board Austan Goolsbee in an interview with ProPublica. "If you don't trust the government, you don't have to do it."

A year later, ProPublica published additional research on Intuit's controversial lobbying actions, claiming that the company had used letters and op-eds from different citizens in order to bolster their arguments against return-free filing. The citizens in question included a rabbi, the mayor of a small town, and a state NAACP official, who were all persuaded by Intuit employees to write letters to Congress that voiced their opposition to the return-free filing system. The aforementioned Intuit employees were connected to Intuit by their association with the Computer & Communications Industry Association (CCIA), of which Intuit is a member. "We think it's important to help policymakers and the public understand what many already know: ReturnFree is unfair, unworkable, and unwise," said CCIA President Ed Black.

It turns out, however, that the individuals who approached the unsuspecting letter-writers were lobbyists for Intuit, meaning that they most likely manipulated the rabbi, mayor, and NAACP official into sending the letters to Congress. "We may have to retract so far based on my research," said NAACP Delaware State Conference president Richard Smith, who was approached by a friend who convinced him to write a letter opposing return-free filing. "I didn't question her."

The same thing happened with other letter-writers. They were approached by various lobbyists and persuaded to write letters to Congress that expressed their concerns with return-free filing. Many of the letter-writers admitted to not doing their research when it came to the benefits of return-free filing. "There's some homework needed," confessed Dennis Huang, executive director of the Asian Business Association. Huang wrote an op-ed in a journal that asserted that return-free filing would disadvantage Asian

American taxpayers.

In March of 2021, Courthouse News Service announced that the $40 million class action settlement against Intuit was rejected. The class action settlement came about after TurboTax was accused of swindling its patrons into paying for services that they could've got for free. U.S. District Judge Charles Breyer of the Northern District of California voiced his opposition to the settlement, saying that it wasn't fair to those who had been affected by TurboTax's greedy actions. "In particular, the proposed settlement provides class members with inadequate compensation and sets forth opt out procedures that unduly burden all class members, but especially those who have already begun to pursue claims through arbitration," wrote Breyer.

If this settlement were to pass, each wronged consumer would only receive around $28, an laughable amount that doesn't compare to how much they were tricked into paying. Judge Breyer slammed TurboTax in a response to the low compensation. "It also bears emphasizing that here, that harm is significant. Mostly low-income class members suffered at least $100 in damages," Breyer wrote. "For class members who paid filing fees over multiple years, the harm was much more. And for a family or individual with limited disposable income, $100-per-year can have a material effect. It might be the difference in whether someone can pay rent for a month or buy groceries for a week."

As you can tell, Intuit has gone through great lengths to ensure that they remain at the top of the food chain. Their latest attempt at draining as much money as possible from their customers' pockets is the Intuit TurboTax Free Edition service.

Let Me Be Clear

It's free to use the basic services of the Intuit TurboTax Free Edition service, but at some point or another, there will be something that pops on the screen that will tell you to pay a fee for an exclusive part of the service. These pop-ups will most likely be an exclusive service that you would need to file your taxes or you would really want to use for your circumstance, such as filing as unemployed, self-employed, or want maximum deductions. This is what makes the Free Edition "not free".

Intuit has pushed this "free" edition in all of its advertising campaigns, going so far as to call the ad campaign "free, free free free." In an Intuit powerpoint that investigated customer calls and complaints, one of the bullet points read, "The website lists Free, Free, Free and the customers are assuming their return will be free." I wonder where the consumers are getting that idea, Intuit. Could it be that they think they won't have to pay for a service that is advertised as free? Other bullet points on the slide mentioned instances of customers accidentally upgrading to a paid-for version of Intuit's tax software, as well as complaints aimed at agents who keep suggesting costly upgrades for people who don't need them. In a statement provided to ProPublica, Intuit spokesperson defended Intuit's stance in regards to government-facilitated filing systems. "We empower our customers to take control of their financial lives, which includes being in charge of their own tax preparation," he said. The spokesperson continued, saying that a "government-run pre-filled tax preparation system that makes the tax collector (who is also the investigator, auditor and enforcer) the tax preparer is fraught with conflicts of interest." He failed to mention that Intuit also has conflicts of interest, as letting the government have their own tax filing software would drive business away from Intuit and into the arms of the IRS, thereby decreasing their profits.

When the IRS got close to establishing its own tax filing system, Intuit took their complaints to the White House, where they accused the IRS of attempting to interfere with private companies. The IRS feared that their funding might be cut. IRS worker Terry Lutes posed the question: "Is there some way to come out of this with something for taxpayers that addresses the administration's objective and at the same time is acceptable to industry?"

And thus a deal was made between the IRS and Intuit. TurboTax would offer free tax filing services to low-income taxpayers and the IRS would not create their own tax filing software. This way, TurboTax would prove their claim that poor taxpayers would be better off without government intervention and the IRS wouldn't have to fear that funding would be withdrawn or that they wouldn't be able to handle the influx of customers and their tax returns.

ic *Their IRS Free File Program, on the other hand, despite being a part of Intuit, is actually free.*

The IRS partnered with Intuit in order to have software that is simple and inexpensive. If you search IRS Free File into the search engine, you'll be taken to the official IRS website. Once you're there, you'll have the opportunity to pick the form that best fits your situation. There is an option for people who have an income of $72,000 and below. The other option is for those who have an income that exceeds $72,000. What exactly is the IRS Free File program? According to the official website, "The IRS Free File Program is a public-private partnership between the IRS and many tax preparation and filing software industry leaders who provide their brand-name products for free." The program debuted in 2003 and has since saved taxpayers an estimated $1.7 billion in application fees.

The program provides two types of federal income tax forms for taxpayers to fill out. The first is the Traditional IRS Free File. This option "provides free online tax preparation and filing options on IRS partner sites," says the government official website. "Our partners are online tax preparation companies that develop and deliver this service at no cost to qualifying taxpayers. Please note, only taxpayers whose adjusted gross income (or AGI) is $72,000 or less qualify for any IRS Free File partner offers." The second option is called the Free File Fillable Forms. These forms are "electronic federal tax forms you can fill out and file online for free. If you choose this option, you should know how to prepare your own tax return. Please note, it is the only IRS Free File option available for taxpayers whose income (AGI) is greater than $72,000." So, the choice between Traditional IRS Free File and the Free File Fillable Forms should be simple, as it all depends on your annual income.

The website also provides taxpayers with some helpful resources, such as information regarding safety, the IRS's partnership with various tax preparation companies, when and where to file, and a list of all of the documents that you need to get started. There is also a place on the website where you can check your filing status by answering a few questions regarding your marital status and household costs. The process takes only 5 minutes and will help determine your "filing requirements, standard deduction, eligibility for certain credits, and your correct tax." There are also resources for students, employees, military members, parents, and seniors who need help filing their taxes.

In order to get started on your IRS Free File, you're going to need a few essential items that include income and receipts, valid social security numbers for all family members, ACA filers, and W-2 forms. IRS Free File requires your tax returns for the current year only, as tax returns from previous years must be filed by registered tax preparers for two years prior. After filing your IRS Free File, you'll receive an email when the IRS has accepted your tax returns.

The Traditional IRS Free File is advertised as "free," but is it actually free? According to the official website, "As long as you qualify for the Free File federal return offer, you must not be charged for preparation and e-filing of a federal tax return. However, state tax preparation fees may apply. Any state preparation or non-qualifying fees must be disclosed on the company's Free File landing page." So, for the most part, the answer is yes.

Little did they know that Intuit would still make it harder for that tax prep service, despite being linked to them, in order to make more money off of the American people, which brings me to my next point below.

THE TAX PREP INDUSTRY WANTS TO MAKE MONEY OFF AMERICANS

Like I stated before, services like Intuit TurboTax like to trick people into using their services by labeling them as "free". Yet, when you go on to their websites, you begin to realize that a lot of the services aren't free.

For the services that are free though, like, through the IRS program, you barely see them when you type "free tax prep services" into a search engine. I tried searching it on Bing and ended up having to scroll towards the bottom to find the program. Oddly enough though, they don't even emphasize the word free when you scroll to it. You would have to click on it and look around before you figure out it is actually a free service. With other non-free services, they have "free" in big letters everywhere. Between the two, which one would you click on? Obviously, the one that says free all over it.

In an article by ProPublica, tax services TurboTax and H&R Block were investigated for their shady search engine secrets and misleading advertisements. Apparently, TurboTax creator Intuit has been attempting to hide the free edition of TurboTax from google search results. They have been doing this by adding a line of code that dubs the free TurboTax website as one that is for internal use only, which would hide it from search results. The code reads "noindex, nofollow," meaning that if someone searches for the website, they aren't going to be able to find it using a search engine. Why would they do this? Well, TurboTax already has a "free" version that is advertised all over their website. The thing is however, this version isn't really free. Though giant wording that reads "FREE Guaranteed" will greet you when you open the TurboTax website, you're going to end up spending money. Despite the fact that 70% of taxpayers qualify to use the TurboTax Free File program, only 3% of them actually used it. They wanted to hide their actual free version because, when it comes down to it, TurboTax just wants to make a profit.

A similar problem arose with Intuit's smaller program, H&R Block. Like the TurboTax Free File, the H&R Block Free File was hidden from Google search results. When questioned about the matter, a H&R spokesperson replied: "We are proud that we have helped millions of Americans file their returns under the Free File Alliance program. ... Our Free File Alliance offering, like all other alliance partners, is presented in the IRS site and easily reachable through the IRS, on HRBlock.com, and also by googling 'FFA H&R Block.'" But this spokesperson is stretching the truth. The H&R Block Free File program isn't exactly easily reachable because the search results don't take you directly to the program's page. U.S. Representative Katie Porter contacted IRS Commissioner Charles Rettig and asked him and his team to investigate both TurboTax and H&R Block's code in order to determine if it was actually preventing taxpayers from seeing the Free File website in search results. As a result of her actions, Intuit has now removed the line of code that had hidden the Free File websites from search results. Now, the truly free TurboTax and H&R Block programs should be prominently shown whenever you search for them on any search engine.

TurboTax was also under fire in 2019 for its exploitation of military service members. TurboTax tricked men and women in uniform into filing their taxes using their TurboTax Military program rather than their actually free TurboTax Free File program. They laid the bait for the trap by heavily promoting patriotic messages, advertising their TurboTax Military program as one that would be the best option for veterans. The truth is, however, that the program isn't the best option. In fact, military members ended up paying money for the TurboTax Military program when they would be better off opting for the TurboTax Free File program, which is completely free. When you file your taxes through TurboTax Military, you'll only receive a $5 discount on charges that are nearly $200, whereas the TurboTax Free File program costs $0 for the same services. "I am upset and troubled that TurboTax would intentionally mislead members of the military," said Petty Officer Laurell, who served in the United States Navy for over a decade.

"Intuit has long supported active-military and veterans, both in filing their taxes and in their communities, overseas, and in the Intuit workplace," said Intuit spokesman Rick Heineman in a statement. "Intuit is proud to support active military, including the millions of men and women in uniform who have filed their tax returns completely free using TurboTax." However, TurboTax's actions haven't lined up with their words. The military discount is still being advertised as the best option for veterans when it comes to filing their taxes. A class action was recently filed against TurboTax in hopes of getting retribution for the money the company has charged military service members. Hopefully, TurboTax will amend their wrongs and do better to ensure that veterans get the best possible service - even if that means making a little less money.

TurboTax's military discount fiasco is just another example of how tax filing companies try to get you to use their "free" services instead of actual *free* services.

DISPROPORTIONATELY AUDITS POORER CITIZENS

What exactly is a tax audit? According to the IRS website, "An IRS audit is a review/examination of an organization's or individual's accounts and financial information to ensure information is reported correctly according to the tax laws and to verify the reported amount of tax is correct." People can be selected for an audit for one of two reasons: they were randomly selected by a computer or the IRS has detected an issue with their tax returns. As it is with most things, the IRS highly favors those with bigger bank accounts. If you are selected for an audit, you will be notified by mail. From there, you will either have to provide more information regarding your tax return via mail or a face-to-face interview. During the audit, an IRS representative will ask about certain items on your tax return, such as expenses and income. They will ask to see records and receipts, which is why it is essential to keep such things in a safe place as you collect them throughout the year. You are required to keep all of the materials that you used to fill out your tax returns for at least three years. This is important because the IRS can include tax returns filed three years prior in the audit. "Generally, the IRS can include returns filed within the last three years in an audit. If we identify a substantial error, we may add additional years. We usually don't go back more than the last six years."

There are three outcomes to an IRS audit: no change, agreed, and disagreed. No change means that you have provided the IRS with sufficient evidence and are free to move on with your life. Agreed means that the person being audited has agreed to the changes proposed by the IRS. Disagreed means that they have disagreed with the changes proposed by the IRS. A person who has disagreed will need to meet with an IRS manager or file an appeal, but it all depends on how much time is left on the audit. If you are ever audited by the IRS, it's important to know your rights as a taxpayer. As a taxpayer, you have the right to "professional and courteous treatment by IRS employees," "know why the IRS is asking for information, how the IRS will use it and what will happen if the requested information is not provided," "privacy and confidentiality about tax matters," and "appeal disagreements, both within the IRS and before the courts," among other things. You can go to the IRS's website and access Publication 1 in order to read the complete lists of rights.

How can you avoid being audited by the IRS? Though there are many tips out there when it comes to minimizing your chance at being selected for an IRS audit, there is no way to be completely sure that you won't be audited. That is because a very small percentage of IRS audits are random. Yes, that means you could be in the very small group of unlucky people who get audited for no particular reason. However, there's no need to fret, as the percentage of people who are randomly selected for an audit is miniscule. So, how can you do your part to avoid actually being selected for an audit? Well, there are plenty of red flags that you should steer clear of when filing your taxes. Doing so will make your tax record squeaky-clean and spot-free, greatly decreasing your chances at catching the attention of the IRS.

One mistake that you should be sure to avoid is failing to accurately report your taxable income. Though the idea of omitting a few sources of income may seem attractive, it can have dire consequences. Under-reporting your taxable income is a mistake that will most certainly be caught by the IRS. According to the official IRS website, "The IRS receives information from third parties, such as employers and financial institutions. Using an automated system, the Automated Underreporter (AUR) function compares the information reported by third parties to the information reported on your return to identify potential discrepancies. When a potential discrepancy is identified, a tax examiner further reviews the return, comparing the information reported to the IRS by employers, banks, businesses, and other payers on income documents (Forms W-2, 1098, 1099, etc.) to the income, credits, and deductions you report on your income tax return." No matter how many sources of income you have or where that income comes from, it's important to report them on your tax forms lest you want an audit request from the IRS.

Another mistake to avoid is overestimating the amount of charitable donations that you made. In addition to being a good thing to do, charitable donations are a great way to decrease the amount of money that you have to pay to the IRS. However, the IRS will question any listed donations that aren't backed up by sufficient proof. In fact, the IRS knows just how much money the average person in your income bracket donates to charity each year, so red flags will be raised as soon as you cross the threshold. This isn't to say that you shouldn't be donating a large amount to charity. You can still donate as much money as your heart desires, but it's important to keep receipts so that your donations are backed up with ample, unquestionable proof. It's also important to pay attention to the different requirements depending on how much money you've donated. "If you claim a deduction of more than $500, but not more than $5,000 per item (or a group of similar items), you must fill out Form 8283, Section A," says the IRS website. "If you claim a deduction of more than $5,000 per item (or a group of similar items), you must obtain a qualified appraisal of the item or group of items and fill out Form 8283, Section B. If you claim a deduction of more than $500,000 for a contribution of noncash property, you must fill out Form 8283, Section B, and also attach the qualified appraisal to your return."

Another IRS red flag has to do with the Home Office Deduction. In order to qualify for the Home Office Deduction, you must either conduct business only at your home or have part of your home reserved exclusively for doing work on a regular basis. The Tax Cuts and Jobs Act has suspended the business use of the Home Office Deduction until 2025, so if you receive a W-2 from an employer, you are not eligible for the deduction. Although nearly everyone had to work from home during the 2020 Covid-19 pandemic, most of them weren't eligible for the Home Office Deduction. That's because they were still receiving income from employers. There are two methods to determine the amount that you can deduct via the Home Office Deduction. The first method, called the regular method, requires that "qualifying taxpayers compute the business use of home deduction by dividing expenses of operating the home between personal and business use. Self-employed taxpayers filing IRS Schedule C, Profit or Loss from Business (Sole Proprietorship) first figure this deduction on Form 8829, Expenses for Business Use of Your Home." The second method, called the simplified method, requires that "qualifying taxpayers use a prescribed rate of $5 per square foot of the portion of the home used for business (up to a maximum of 300 square feet) to figure the business use of home deduction. A taxpayer claims the deduction directly on IRS Schedule C. Revenue Procedure 2013-13 provides complete details of this safe harbor method." Whichever method you choose to use, it's important to be honest when it comes to how much you actually spent on your home office. The IRS is extra perceptive when it comes to overestimations related to home office work because it has a history of catching home office miscalculations.

One tip to help make your tax return less likely to be selected for an audit is to use a Schedule C when reporting small business losses or income. "Always report all small business earnings using Schedule C," says CEO of True Contrarian Investments Steven Jon Kaplan. "Although there are other methods which may sometimes avoid paying part of your Medicare tax or have other advantages, they also greatly increase the likelihood of an audit."

Most people who are self-employed will be required to fill out the Schedule C form. Unfortunately, the IRS will be looking closely at Schedule C forms for any mistakes made or liberties taken when it comes to the amount of tax-deductions listed. A mistake that people who run small businesses often make is taking deductions for business meals and travel. Spending a suspiciously high amount on meals and travel for "business" is going to raise alarms, so it's always a good idea to not overdo it when taking these types of deductions. If you are a professional gambler, you are required to report losses on the Schedule C form. If you claim excessively large gambling losses or fail to report gambling wins, you have a high chance of being contacted by an IRS representative for an audit. A red flag may also be raised if you report day-trading losses on your Schedule C form. While expenses of traders are deductible, the expenses of investors are not, so many times investors try to parade as traders in order to get a higher deductible. Because the IRS knows that investors tend to do this, they will be extra observant when reviewing Schedule C forms filed by traders.

ProPublica has investigated the IRS and written multiple articles that call the IRS's practices into question. When lawmakers began to take notice of the IRS's disparity when it comes to who they audit, they called upon IRS Commissioner Charles Rettig to correct the issue. In September of 2019, Rettig replied with a letter.

"The IRS cannot simply shift examination resources from single issue correspondence audits to more complex higher income audits because of employee experience and skill set," explained Rettig. "A GS-B tax examiner is not trained to conduct a high income, high wealth taxpayer audit. In order to increase parity of numbers of taxpayers audited, the IRS must reallocate high-graded resources from certain issues to high income, high wealth taxpayer returns. Further, the rate of attrition is significantly higher among these more experienced examiners. It is also important to maintaining the voluntary compliance level that the IRS has an audit presence across all income groups, including EITC."

In short, Rettig justified the IRS's unfairness by citing their employees lack of training, the difficulty of auditing people with higher income, and how the IRS lacks sufficient funding. Senator Ron Wyden of Oregon was one of the prominent politicians to hold the IRS and Charles Rettig accountable. When he read Rettig's letter, his reply was congruent to Rettig's concerns about the funding of the IRS, "but that does not eliminate the need for the agency to begin reversing the alarming trend of plummeting audit rates of the wealthy within its current budget."

There have been other studies conducted that show just how rampant inequality is when it comes to who the IRS chooses to audit. According to ProPublica, a person earning an annual income of $20,000 is more likely to be audited than a person earning an annual income of $400,000. In their article, ProPublica shared the story of 28-year-old Natassia Smick, a wife and mother who was forced to endure a long and frustrating audit process, all while being a participant in one of the government's broadest anti-poverty programs: EITC.

EITC, which stands for earned income tax credit, is supposed to provide low-income families with a tax break. It ended up being useless to Smick, who received a letter from the IRS four months after submitting her taxes that requested supporting documentation for everything she had listed in her filings. This meant finding the receipts, bank statements, and medical records that the family had accumulated through the years and submitting them to the IRS within 30 days. Smick was confused by the request.

She had used TurboTax, a tax software that was supposed to help limit the number of mistakes in her tax returns. It just didn't make any sense. Smick went through the stressful process of searching through files and sorting through the clutter of home, sending her documents off to the IRS just in the nick of time. How was Smick rewarded for her compliance and efficiency? With a letter from the IRS saying that they would get back to her in six months. Six months! By that time, Natassia and her family could be in financial ruin. When she called the IRS and demanded an explanation, they told her that there was nothing they could do. The IRS admitted that they were "extremely short staffed." They were moving as fast as they could, but her wait time of six months would have to remain in place.

In an interview with ProPublica, Oregon Senator Ron Wyden suggested that the solution to decreasing the unfair audits on the poor might be increasing the number of IRS staff members and decreasing the complexity of tax credit acquisition. "Those struggling to make ends meet are being unfairly audited while the fortunate few dodge taxes without consequence," said Wyden. "The IRS needs more manpower to go after tax cheats of all sizes, and working Americans need a simpler way of obtaining a tax credit they've earned."

A 2020 report showed that poorer taxpayers - those who make less than $25,000 in annual income - have an audit rate of 0.69%. This is over 50% higher than the overall audit rate. Taxpayers within this income range are more likely to get that dreaded audit letter than other income groups. The only group that has a higher audit rate is the group that includes individuals who make over $500,000 per year. But, when it comes down to it, individuals in the poorest income bracket will be more highly affected by the audit than those who have money to spare.

One big reason why poor taxpayers are targeted by the IRS may be related to the Earned Income Tax Credit. Earned Income Tax

Credit is a credit meant to ease the burden of taxes for low-income families. Because the Earned Income Tax Credit comes with many complex rules and regulations, there are often misunderstandings and mistakes on the related forms. This prompts the IRS to pay close attention to the tax returns of families who have participated in the Earned Income Tax Credit program.

"If you are a single parent with multiple children and with income in the $25,000 range, that is likely the person who will likely get the most amount of money from the EITC," says tax expert Eric Bronnenkant. "One of the problems is there is EITC fraud."

According to the Tax Policy Center, "In FY 2018, the IRS audited 1.1 million of the almost 196 million returns filed, less than 1 percent of the total. Returns claiming an earned income tax credit (EITC) were audited at a rate more than twice that of all individual income tax returns: 1.4 percent compared with 0.6 percent. Almost all these audits (94 percent) were correspondence audits, meaning the tax filer was notified and could respond by mail." Why are people who claim the Earned Income Tax Credit audited at such a high rate? It should be that the more money you make, the more likely you are to be under scrutiny by the IRS. So why are people in the lowest income bracket being audited the most? There are many factors, but one of the most likely is that the IRS is worried about "improper payments." The Earned Income Tax Credit is one of the few credits that don't require an application. Instead, any taxpayer can claim the credit without being forced to go through an approval process. Because of this, there have been claims that too much money has been granted.

The wealthier Americans within the country usually have multiple streams of income from multiple investments and jobs. So, you would think that with all that money moving around them that the IRS would keep a closer eye on their income. Yet, they don't. I can only assume that they choose to not focus on the wealthier Americans because those Americans are able to afford the best accountants. These accountants make sure that their clients are able to have maximum deductions while making sure all their income is filed. Obviously, poorer or even middle-class Americans can't afford these types of accountants, so they either end up getting someone cheap or inexperienced to do it or just doing it themselves. Through these methods of filing taxes, I would then assume that more mistakes would occur, unlike with the wealthier people.

Since it is unknown why poorer people are audited more often than weather ones, I cannot say if these assumptions are true, but I'm sure that they are not far from it.

WHAT COULD MAKE IT BETTER?

There are many deep-rooted and systemic issues that inhibit poor people from having accessibility to the same resources as people who are wealthy. Taxes would be so much easier to file if the tax prep industry wasn't so money hungry and if the IRS's free program had better marketing, so Americans would know it better. It also wouldn't hurt if poorer Americans had greater access to more secure services in order to avoid frequent auditing.

Will these things ever happen? I don't know. Be sure to contact your local government officials and legislatures to let them know about your concerns. Hopefully one day more Americans could realize these truths and take them to their local government to petition or urge them to do something for the people. I know I sure hope so.

www.ingramcontent.com/pod-product-compliance
Lightning Source LLC
Chambersburg PA
CBHW070906220526
45466CB00005B/2151